Snippets of Oscar Wilde

DAVE FARNHAM

DISCLAIMER

While every effort has been made to ensure the information in this book is correct, human error is always a possibility and therefore the author cannot accept responsibility for any inaccuracies.

CONTENTS

INTRODUCTION

Oscar Wilde seemed to have everything he needed to make a success of his life: born into a prosperous family where he was well loved, he received a first -class education, learned to speak fluently in French and German, graduated from Dublin and Oxford with honours and was a hit in London's fashionable society.

He wrote poetry, stories, newspaper and magazine articles as well as plays, all of which were enthusiastically. His wit and wonderful way with words marked him out, not just in his own era but for succeeding generations, too. He married a intelligent woman with her own income and had two children.

But at the point where he should have been able to reap the rewards of his success he made the mistake of taking a lawsuit out against the Marquess of Queensberry, with whose son he was having an illicit affair, and his life fell apart. He spent two years in prison and came out a broken man, spending his remaining days in poverty in

France.

But though his life ended in tragedy, his writings still continue to give pleasure to millions, particularly his play *The Importance Of Being Earnest*, in which his effervescent sense of humour is at its liveliest.

In this book you will find Oscar Wilde's amusing musings on many subjects as well as some of his more serious thoughts, all of which should give you plenty to think about, laugh at and enjoy.

BIO

Oscar Wilde

Full name: Oscar Fingal O'Flahertie Wills Wilde

1854 October 16th Born in Dublin to Sir William and Lady Jane Wilde. Older brother William (known as Willie). Father was a noted ear and eye surgeon as well as a writer and philanthropist. Mother was a poet who wrote under the pen-name Speranza.

1857 April 2nd Birth of sister, Isola Francesca Emily. Oscar was educated at home until the age of nine and learned French and German form live-in tutors.

1863 Attended Portora Royal School, Enniskillen.

1866 February, Isola died from meningitis.

1871 – 1874 Oscar was a awarded scholarship and

3

studied Classics at Trinity College, Dublin, where he developed a lifelong love of all things Greek. He shared rooms there with his brother Willie. Graduated with the highest honours.

1874 – 1878 Studied "Greats" (Oxford's name for Classics) at Magdalen College, Oxford. Won the 1878 Newdigate prize for his poem *Ravenna*. Graduated with a double first.

1876 Death of Oscar's father.

1878 Returned to Dublin but, following the death of his childhood sweetheart to Bram Stoker, decided to leave again for England and settled in Chelsea, London and concentrated on writing poetry.

1881 Published his first volume of poetry under the title of *Poems*, with moderate success.

1882 Travelled to New York to give lectures across America – 140 in nine months, on a variety of artistic subjects including interior design. His lectures were very well received.

1884 May 29th In London, he married Constance Lloyd, a Queen's Counsellor. They had two sons, Cyril (1885 – 1915) and Vyvyan (1886 – 1967).

1887 Appointed editor of *The Lady's World* magazine, which he renamed *The Woman's World*, wanting to write about deeper issues that concerned women than just fashion.

1888 Published *The Happy Prince And Other Tales*.

1889 Left *The Woman's World*, bored of being an editor, and turned instead to writing articles for a number of magazines.

1891 Published his novel *The Picture of Dorian Gray*. The same year he was introduced to Alfred Douglas, an Oxford undergraduate and son of the Marquess of Queensberry. Wilde became infatuated with Alfred.

1891 Went to Paris to meet many literary figures in French society and was received as a celebrity. Whilst there he wrote *Salome*, in French. It could not be performed in England because of its portrayal of Biblical characters, forbidden at the time. It was finally performed in Paris in 1896.

1892 His play *Lady Windermere's Fan*, was first performed. A satire on Victorian Society masked as comedy, it was a great success.

1893 He became deeply embroiled in an affair with Alfred Douglas and involved in London's gay life.

1894 Wrote his play *The Importance Of Being Earnest*, his most popular and enduring work. It was first performed the following year and was an immediate triumph.

 1895 The Marquess of Queensberry accused Wilde of sodomy. Wilde, despite his friends' advice, took libel action against him. The Marquess' lawyers hired private detectives to prove his accusations. During the trial Wilde decided to drop the charges, as much evidence was working against him. This was taken as a sign of his guilt. The Marques was acquitted and an arrest warrant taken out against Oscar Wilde who was arrested at the Cadogan Hotel, Knightsbridge, London. At the subsequent trial he was found guilty of sodomy and gross indecency and sentenced to two years' hard labour. He was imprisoned first in Pentonville, then Wandsworth, before being transferred to Reading Gaol. His health suffered greatly.

1897 Wrote *De Profundis* ('from the depths'), a fifty-thousand word letter to Alfred Douglas, which was published in 1905. It dealt with his feelings about his time in prison. He was released on May 19th and left England to spend the rest of his life in France., where he wrote his poem *The Ballad Of Reading Gaol*.

1900 Died, at the age of 46, in poverty in the Hotel d'Alsace in Paris. He was buried in the Bagneux cemetery but later disinterred and transferred to the Père Lachaise Cemetery, where his tomb was designed by sculptor Jacob Epstein.

ABOUT HIMSELF

"I choose my friends for their good looks, my acquaintances for their good characters, and my enemies for their intellects. A man cannot be too careful in the choice of his enemies."

*

"If you are not too long, I will wait here for you all my life."

*

"I am not young enough to know everything."

*

"I want my food dead. Not sick, not dying, dead."

*

"I have the simplest tastes. I am always satisfied with the best."

*

"I always pass on good advice. It is the only thing to do with it. It is never of any use to oneself."

*

"I am the only person in the world I should like to know thoroughly."

*

"The only way to get rid of temptation is to yield to it... I can resist everything but temptation."

*

"I am so clever that sometimes I don't understand a single word of what I am saying."

*

"I have nothing to declare except my genius."

*

"When I was young I thought that money was the most important thing in life; now that I am old I know that it is."

*

"Whenever people agree with me I always feel I must be wrong."

*

"This suspense is terrible. I hope it will last."

*

When first I was put into prison some people advised me to try and forget who I was. It was ruinous advice. It is only by realising what I am that I have found comfort of any kind. Now I am advised by others to try on my release to forget that I have ever been in a prison at all. I know that would be equally fatal. It would mean that I would always be haunted by an intolerable sense of disgrace, and that those things that are meant for me as much as for anybody else – the beauty of the sun and moon, the pageant of the seasons, the music of daybreak and the silence of great nights, the rain falling through the leaves, or the dew creeping over the grass and making it silver – would all be tainted for me, and lose their healing power, and their power of communicating joy. To regret one's own experiences is to arrest one's own development. To deny one's own experiences is to put a lie into the lips of one's own life. It is no less than a denial of the soul.

ABOUT PEOPLE

"Fathers should be neither seen nor heard. That is the
only proper basis for family life."

*

"Man can believe the impossible, but man can never
believe the improbable."

*

"How can a woman be expected to be happy with a man
who insists on treating her as if she were a perfectly
normal human being?"

*

"Arguments are extremely vulgar, for everyone in good society holds exactly the same opinion."

*

"Whenever a man does a thoroughly stupid thing, it is always from the noblest motives."

*

"Democracy means simply the bludgeoning of the people by the people for the people."

*

"What is a cynic? A man who knows the price of everything and the value of nothing."

*

"Selfishness is not living as one wishes to live, it is asking others to live as one wishes to live."

*

"There are many things that we would throw away if we
were not afraid that others might pick them up."

*

"It is only by not paying one's bills that one can hope to
live in the memory of the commercial classes."

*

"Ridicule is the tribute paid to the genius by the
mediocrities."

*

"Everybody who is incapable of learning has taken to
teaching."

*

"No woman should ever be quite accurate about her age.
It looks so calculating."

*

"As long as a woman can look ten years younger than her own daughter, she is perfectly satisfied."

*

"Only the shallow know themselves."

*

"There is always something infinitely mean about other people's tragedies."

*

"Woman begins by resisting a man's advances and ends by blocking his retreat."

*

"Women are never disarmed by compliments. Men always are. That is the difference between the sexes."

*

"The public is wonderfully tolerant. It forgives everything except genius."

*

"True friends stab you in the front."

*

"There are only two kinds of people who are really fascinating - people who know absolutely everything, and people who know absolutely nothing."

*

"Mr. Henry James writes fiction as if it were a painful duty."

*

"There is only one class in the community that thinks more about money than the rich, and that is the poor. The poor can think of nothing else."

*

"The old believe everything, the middle-aged suspect everything, the young know everything."

*

"Pessimist: One who, when he has the choice of two evils, chooses both."

*

"One can survive everything, nowadays, except death, and live down everything except a good reputation."

*

"The salesman knows nothing of what he is selling save that he is charging a great deal too much for it."

*

"Some cause happiness wherever they go; others whenever they go."

*

"Man is a rational animal who always loses his temper when he is called upon to act in accordance with the dictates of reason."

*

"Society exists only as a mental concept; in the real world there are only individuals."

*

"Work is the curse of the drinking classes."

*

"When good Americans die they go to Paris."

*

"Children begin by loving their parents; after a time they judge them; rarely, if ever, do they forgive them."

*

"Why was I born with such contemporaries?"

*

"A gentleman is one who never hurts anyone's feelings unintentionally."

*

"Most people die of a sort of creeping common sense, and discover when it is too late that the only things one never regrets are one's mistakes."

*

"The man who can dominate a London dinner-table can dominate the world."

*

"All women become like their mothers. That is their tragedy. No man does. That's his."

*

"An excellent man; he has no enemies; and none of his friends like him."

*

"It is absurd to divide people into good and bad. People are either charming or tedious."

*

"Man is least himself when he talks in his own person. Give him a mask, and he will tell you the truth."

*

"If one plays good music, people don't listen and if one plays bad music people don't talk."

*

"Seriousness is the only refuge of the shallow."

*

"I suppose society is wonderfully delightful. To be in it is merely a bore. But to be out of it is simply a tragedy."

*

"The well bred contradict other people. The wise

contradict themselves."

*

"A dreamer is one who can only find his way by moonlight, and his punishment is that he sees the dawn before the rest of the world."

*

"Most people are other people. Their thoughts are someone else's opinions, their lives a mimicry, their passions a quotation."

*

"The only difference between the saint and the sinner is that every saint has a past, and every sinner has a future."

*

"If one could only teach the English how to talk, and the Irish how to listen, society here would be quite civilized."

*

"The world is divided into two classes, those who believe the incredible, and those who do the improbable."

*

"A man's face is his autobiography. A woman's face is her work of fiction."

*

"Between men and women there is no friendship possible. There is passion, enmity, worship, love, but no friendship."

*

"A man who does not think for himself does not think at all."

ABOUT AMERICA

"America had often been discovered before Columbus,
but it had always been hushed up."

*

"In America the young are always ready to give to those
who are older than themselves the full benefits of their
inexperience."

*

"America is the only country that went from barbarism
to decadence without civilization in between."

*

"Perhaps, after all, America never has been discovered. I myself would say that it had merely been detected."

*

"In America the President reigns for four years, and Journalism governs forever and ever."

ABOUT ART

"Art is the most intense mode of individualism that the world has known."

*

"No great artist ever sees things as they really are. If he did, he would cease to be an artist."

*

"The moment you think you understand a great work of art, it's dead for you."

*

"The critic has to educate the public; the artist has to educate the critic."

*

"It is through art, and through art only, that we can realise our perfection."

*

"Every portrait that is painted with feeling is a portrait of the artist, not of the sitter."

*

"A work of art is the unique result of a unique temperament."

*

"It is only an auctioneer who can equally and impartially admire all schools of art."

*

"All art is quite useless."

ABOUT BOOKS & WRITING

"All bad poetry springs from genuine feeling."

*

"If one cannot enjoy reading a book over and over again,
there is no use in reading it at all."

*

"The books that the world calls immoral are books that
show the world its own shame."

*

"It is always the unreadable that occurs."

*

"The good ended happily, and the bad unhappily. That is what fiction means."

*

"A poet can survive everything but a misprint."

*

"The difference between literature and journalism is that journalism is unreadable and literature is not read."

*

"It is what you read when you don't have to that determines what you will be when you can't help it."

*

"By giving us the opinions of the uneducated, journalism keeps us in touch with the ignorance of the community."

*

"Biography lends to death a new terror."

*

"There is no such thing as a moral or an immoral book. Books are well written, or badly written."

ABOUT LIFE

"There is something terribly morbid in the modern sympathy with pain. One should sympathise with the colour, the beauty, the joy of life. The less said about life's sores the better."

*

"The true mystery of the world is the visible, not the invisible."

*

"In modern life nothing produces such an effect as a good platitude. It makes the whole world kin."

*

"One's past is what one is. It is the only way by which people should be judged."

*

"Life imitates art far more than art imitates Life."

*

"Life is far too important a thing ever to talk seriously about."

*

"It is only the modern that ever becomes old-fashioned."

*

"The world is a stage, but the play is badly cast."

*

"There is only one thing in life worse than being talked

about, and that is not being talked about."

*

"One's real life is so often the life that one does not lead."

*

"One of the many lessons that one learns in prison is, that things are what they are and will be what they will be."

*

"No man is rich enough to buy back his past."

*

"Life is never fair, and perhaps it is a good thing for most of us that it is not."

*

"There are only two tragedies in life: one is not getting what one wants, and the other is getting it."

ABOUT LOVE, MARRIAGE & ROMANCE

"I see when men love women. They give them but a little of their lives. But women when they love give everything."

*

"The world has grown suspicious of anything that looks like a happily married life."

*

"Men marry because they are tired; women, because they are curious; both are disappointed."

*

"A man can be happy with any woman, as long as he does not love her."

*

"Romance should never begin with sentiment. It should begin with science and end with a settlement."

*

"There is nothing so difficult to marry as a large nose."

*

"Men always want to be a woman's first love - women like to be a man's last romance."

*

"The one charm about marriage is that it makes a life of deception absolutely necessary for both parties."

*

"Those whom the gods love grow young."

*

"Keep love in your heart. A life without it is like a sunless garden when the flowers are dead."

*

"One should always be in love. That is the reason one should never marry."

*

"When a man has once loved a woman he will do anything for her except continue to love her."

*

"While we look to the dramatist to give romance to realism, we ask of the actor to give realism to romance."

*

"There is always something ridiculous about the

emotions of people whom one has ceased to love."

*

"Who, being loved, is poor?"

*

"Deceiving others. That is what the world calls a romance."

*

"Bigamy is having one wife too many. Monogamy is the same."

*

"There's nothing in the world like the devotion of a married woman. It's a thing no married man knows anything about."

*

"In married life three is company and two none."

*

"To love oneself is the beginning of a lifelong romance."

*

"How marriage ruins a man! It is as demoralizing as cigarettes, and far more expensive."

*

"Women are made to be loved, not understood."

GENERAL PHILOSOPHY

"Our ambition should be to rule ourselves, the true kingdom for each one of us; and true progress is to know more, and be more, and to do more."

*

"It is a very sad thing that nowadays there is so little useless information."

*

"Ambition is the germ from which all growth of nobleness proceeds."

*

"The truth is rarely pure and never simple."

*

"There is no sin except stupidity."

*

"Always forgive your enemies - nothing annoys them so much."

*

"As long as war is regarded as wicked, it will always have its fascination. When it is looked upon as vulgar, it will cease to be popular."

*

"Everything popular is wrong."

*

"An idea that is not dangerous is unworthy of being

called an idea at all."

*

"You will always be fond of me. I represent to you all the sins you have never had the courage to commit."

*

"Memory... is the diary that we all carry about with us."

*

"Ambition is the last refuge of the failure."

*

"Now that the House of Commons is trying to become useful, it does a great deal of harm."

*

"Ordinary riches can be stolen; real riches cannot. In your soul are infinitely precious things that cannot be taken from you."

*

"A thing is not necessarily true because a man dies for it."

*

"The imagination imitates. It is the critical spirit that creates."

*

"Morality is simply the attitude we adopt towards people whom we personally dislike."

*

"Consistency is the last refuge of the unimaginative."

*

"Nothing can cure the soul but the senses, just as nothing can cure the senses but the soul."

*

"The typewriting machine, when played with expression, is no more annoying than the piano when played by a sister or near relation."

*

"To lose one parent may be regarded as a misfortune; to lose both looks like carelessness."

*

"Questions are never indiscreet, answers sometimes are."

*

"Patriotism is the virtue of the vicious."

*

"No object is so beautiful that, under certain conditions, it will not look ugly."

*

"I sometimes think that God in creating man somewhat
overestimated his ability."

*

"Death and vulgarity are the only two facts in the
nineteenth century that one cannot explain away."

*

"Do you really think it is weakness that yields to
temptation? I tell you that there are terrible temptations
which it requires strength, strength and courage to yield
to."

*

"A little sincerity is a dangerous thing, and a great deal
of it is absolutely fatal."

*

"If there was less sympathy in the world, there would be
less trouble in the world."

*

"Laughter is not at all a bad beginning for a friendship, and it is far the best ending for one."

*

"We are all in the gutter, but some of us are looking at the stars."

*

"Experience is one thing you can't get for nothing."

*

"Education is an admirable thing, but it is well to remember from time to time that nothing that is worth knowing can be taught."

*

"There is no necessity to separate the monarch from the mob; all authority is equally bad."

*

"Hatred is blind, as well as love."

*

"The advantage of the emotions is that they lead us astray."

*

"To expect the unexpected shows a thoroughly modern intellect."

*

"Arguments are to be avoided: they are always vulgar and often convincing."

*

"I can stand brute force, but brute reason is quite unbearable. There is something unfair about its use. It is hitting below the intellect."

*

"Conversation about the weather is the last refuge of the unimaginative."

*

"Anybody can be good in the country. There are no temptations there."

*

"If you pretend to be good, the world takes you very seriously. If you pretend to be bad, it doesn't. Such is the astounding stupidity of optimism."

*

"Fashion is a form of ugliness so intolerable that we have to alter it every six months."

*

"It is better to have a permanent income than to be fascinating."

*

"Nothing is so aggravating as calmness."

*

"Illusion is the first of all pleasures."

*

"It is better to be beautiful than to be good. But... it is better to be good than to be ugly."

*

"There is a luxury in self-reproach. When we blame ourselves we feel no one else has a right to blame us."

*

"Experience is simply the name we give our mistakes."

*

"One should always play fairly when one has the winning cards."

*

"Moderation is a fatal thing. Nothing succeeds like excess."

*

"In all matters of opinion, our adversaries are insane."

*

"Success is a science; if you have the conditions, you get the result."

*

"The basis of optimism is sheer terror."

*

"Charity creates a multitude of sins."

*

"When the gods wish to punish us they answer our prayers."

*

"What we have to do, what at any rate it is our duty to do, is to revive the old art of Lying."

ALSO BY DAVE FARNHAM

Snippets of Richard Attenborough

Snippets of Billy Connolly

Snippets of Paul Gascoigne

Snippets of Jeremy Kyle

Snippets of Boris Johnson

Snippets of Nigel Farage

Snippets of Joan Rivers

Gandhi's Teachings for Troubled Times

www.ingramcontent.com/pod-product-compliance
Lightning Source LLC
Chambersburg PA
CBHW060221290526
45789CB00003B/1355